COULD THIS BE YOUR NEXT MOVE?

Modification
Short Sale
Foreclosure
Reverse Mortgage
Option to Buy

Before you make your next move you need to read this book. If you are confused what all these terms mean, you will be confused about the best Real Estate decision for you.

By

Ariana CP Hunter,
Real Estate Broker

2

www.sucasacastillo.com

info@sucasacastillo.com

210- 420-9361

I dedicate this book to my Maker, my parents, husband,
children, and grandson.
In memory of my grandfather Solon Castillo Ruiz
who taught me to love the land and to buy
and keep as much land as I possibly could.

San Antonio, Texas, 2012

4

Chapter 1

My Story

Once upon a time I was a happy real estate agent. I was happy helping people buy the property of their dreams. One day I realized that the market was changing, that there was something very wrong. I worked as a full-service agent representing clients in the sale and purchase of their homes and businesses. I also assisted them in finding the correct loan agent to be able to finance their transactions. After a while, I began to assist clients in obtaining their loans in order to make the transaction smoother and also to make a profit for myself. In California at the time in the early 2000's, it was also allowed for real estate agents to be loan agents. I moved to a company that was mainly a mortgage company. I worked for wonderful people who taught me a lot about how the loan process worked. They were wonderful knowable savvy business people. At that time the market itself was getting crazy. I began to notice all the corruption that was going around me. To be honest it was the first time ever that I took some time to reflect whether it was an industry I wanted to be still part of. I decided that I was not willing and am still not willing to make money by being shady, corrupt. In real estate in order to have what is call a fair transaction, it must be arm's length with all parties that understand what they're doing. I honestly believe that many people who got into mortgages knew they couldn't afford them and what they were doing, and everybody else in the transaction was in line. There were the real estate agents who did not care if their clients were buying junk properties or purchasing properties in faraway places from their jobs. The same real estate agent introduced their clients to lying loan agents.

And of course, the clients who themselves would lie to the real estate person and loan agents. Let me give an example: if you are the client and your real estate person tells you that you should buy a house that costs $1 million, and you make $16 an hour, and that they're going to give you a great fantastic 1% interest loan, you do not have to know anything about real estate to know that is a debt that most likely you will not be able to pay." Many people who got into the real estate market wanted to keep the property for a very little time and then turn around and sell it. But the problem was that everybody got the great idea all at the same time. Then some unethical appraisers would overvalue some of the properties knowing that those properties were not worth what they claimed they were. Keep in mind that is not the same thing to give an interest only loan or Adjustable-Rate Mortgage (ARM) loan to a surgeon intern than to a dishwasher. Because we know for a fact that that surgeon intern is not always going make that same low income at the time but that his/her income will increase once he starts his/her private practice; therefore, they will be able to refinance and pay for the $1 million home, well at least in California.

Back in 2005 I made a drastic decision and moved to Texas. I had no family in Texas and had only visited Texas. I moved to Texas because it is a conservative state. I didn't see much real estate growth as California but the growth was real. Life is not easy in Texas- but it is predictable, realistic, and conservative.

Texas real estate regulations are very tough, one of the toughest in the country; but I was glad to comply with all their requirements because I was disgusted and sick to see how lenient the real estate law enforcement had become in California, but the truth is that the same scenario was happening all over the country. I always told my husband-during long-night debates that the real estate market was crazy out-of-control unrealistic.

I wondered how could people be able to pay their mortgages, make car payments, insurance payments, and other bills and still have good quality of life? I love real estate but I will never overpay for a property nonetheless all the additional stuff that goes with owning a house. During the period of waiting for compliance with Texas state rules I began to work for a big bank in the mortgage collection and foreclosure department. It was one of the greatest experiences that could ever happen to me. I was able to see the consequences of those nasty loans. I felt sad for the people who had them, I knew I was right about those loans and their consequences. I got to see firsthand. I talked to people and learned their problems, as to why they were not able to pay their loans, and I was not surprised honestly- the loans were nasty; the situations were terrible. As a professional I was disgusted to see the procedures that these people would have to go through in order to attempt to get out the loans they couldn't afford. A lot of people were trying to modify; others trying to short sell: and many more who have given up on their way to get foreclosed. Playing the blaming game did not help anyone get through with the situation.

People were yelling, cursing, threatening to sue the bank and everyone else and finally filing for bankrupt did not help. If one tries to keep the property by modifying it or refinancing it, and one cannot get neither, and one could not afford the property: then one should sell. That was my advice. I was really devastated and angry that a lot of people who put their money on their 401 (k) retirement plans for their older years could be facing major losses and financial instability.

Some of these people had speculated in hope of making tons of money in real estate by buying properties thinking that they could turn around and sell them quickly. I would hear things like I cannot pay this mortgage; your bank could come and take this sh@#%. It was a very sad thing to hear. But it is not fair either for people who deposit their savings in banks in order to make money to lose their investment funds because people just don't pay the mortgages. The money people borrow is the money people deposit at the banks. I understood the position of the bank: they were there to make money to pay interest on those deposits. I understood the position of the clients. They felt robbed by the loan agents, real estate agents, and the bank. But the truth is that nobody gets away with anything. Eventually, the greedy, unethical people were no longer getting business nor had any income, and they too had to pay their mortgage so they ended up in the same boat as their clients. Following the nasty loan since its inception, I had another experience. I also had the opportunity to find out what happened once the loans hit the secondary market. I felt like an investigating journalist. I applied for a job with The Federal National Mortgage Association, Fannie Mae just to get to take a look at what happened to these loans.

The position was to manage property files to determine the work needed to make the house marketable again. In this instance, the customer was the bank. They were submitting claims to be paid by Fannie Mae. Now the end of these loans was that the government would pay for them holding the inventory. Eventually, those properties sold, and we all somehow pay for all this. By the way, I did not take the job. I am now happy real estate broker once again not because of all these bad things that happened but because I made the right decision and not being one of those unethical people; I stuck to my guns knowing that sooner or later the fiasco would backfire. Now I have a wonderful opportunity to share with you the solutions and provide you with a better understanding the real estate transactions from several different perspectives.

Now my position these days is that I only represent buyers and hope you understand me why. Even more, I know people in distress put higher pressure and greater scrutiny on their real estate agents. In my opinion, their expectations are unrealistic. If clients and agents alike follow the proper procedures, the success of a short sale will be likely. As a buyer agent, I know the negotiating, understand the bank's expectations and have a lot of leverage to benefit my clients. I just want to mention I love my industry and am always learning. I have different licenses and certificates. I feel it is honest to say that licenses provide the permission to operate in the field; learning inside the industries is what makes me want to be a better real estate broker.

Chapter 2

What is a Short Sale?

A short sale is a transaction in which the lender or bank allows you to sell your home for less than the amount of the loan - even when your mortgage debt is higher than the value of your home.

Note. Most people who are going into foreclosure may have had qualified for a short sale in the past.

The Short Sale process

The actual Short Sale process can take as little as 3 months or as long as 1 year and involves several steps.

The first one is to hire a real estate agent that specializes in short sale.

Secondly, you contact the bank and let it know that you have the intention of selling your property as a short sale and request the short sale package or kit. The package has forms and instructions as to what needs to be provided to the bank. The following are items that a request for short sale typically contains:

Authorization to release information form

Hardship letter

Financial worksheet

Listing agreement

Copies of tax returns (last two years, first two pages only)

Copies of pay stubs (last two pay periods for all borrowers)

Application for pre-foreclosure program or FHA, HUD form 90036

Homeownership counseling form or FHA, HUD form 90038

Signed purchase offer

Buyer's pre-qualification letter from the lender. If cash, proof of funds from the banking institution.

Estimate of closing sheet/HUD 1

CMA (comparative market analysis)

The third step is that real estate agent must conduct a market analysis to determine what the properties are selling for in your neighborhood in order to set the correct price. Usually, this price is more or less 20% below what you currently owe the bank. Setting the correct price could be really tricky because the agents of the bank will never disclose the amount they are willing to accept, so the price of the home has to be a realistic amount the bank will accept. (Just because your home was accepted to be in a short sale it does not mean that you are not responsible for the mortgage. You must still make your mortgage payments while in the process of selling it.)

The fourth step happens when the property goes on the local Multiple Listing Service, MLS. That is when you start waiting to have the offer to buy the property. This is the time that no one can predict how long it will take to get an offer. Just because you need to sell the property quickly, it doesn't mean that buyers are dying to buy. They look around for a good opportunity, a good deal. So the process could take two months to a year. Even if you get an offer after one week into your listing, you still must submit the offer to the bank representative. Keep in mind that your property is not the only file the bank representative has to work on. Usually the bank representative handles about 65 to 75 loans a month. The time frame to obtain a response is usually 7 to 14 days. That is just to give you a yes or no answer. The buyers usually want to know right away if their offer was accepted and become restless when waiting for an answer.

The answer, if the answer is no then you go back to waiting for a buyer or buyers to make offer/offers and you must adapt the price of the property to what you think the bank will accept the second time. If the answer is yes, that is when that actual short sale begins and so do the phone calls between your real estate agent and the bank. In most cases, 60 to 90 phone calls back and forth between them are necessary. That is if you only have one mortgage and not a second mortgage. If that is the case, it becomes a tug of war between the first and second lenders. This time is when you make sure your second mortgage lender will be satisfied with the amount they will receive upon closing of escrow; otherwise, they could continue to pursue you for the second mortgage debt you owe them long after the short sale. Therefore, if you do not make arrangements to pay off the debt, the lender has the right to file a lawsuit against you. Fifth step. The buyer will get between 10 and 30 days to perform (arrange their financing and close escrow). Under current market conditions, closing usually takes 60 to 90 days. So your listing agent must be a good negotiator and communicator to explain the process to the buyer's agent, so the buyer has realistic expectations as for when closing will occur. Along escrow is not a bad thing if the buyers are not in a rush. A short sale is not for the person who needs to move right away within 30 days.

It is very important to only accept a realistic offer for your listing. Your agent will present to you all offers, but you do not have to accept any only the ones you think the bank will take seriously. Not all offers are good offers. How the buyer will pay or finance the property is one of the most important questions the bank file manager will ask. So make sure you do your homework and try to accept an offer that will be not complicated for the bank.

After the closing of escrow, some banks may give you from $3,000 to $5,000 funds for you to vacate and move. That way you do not leave empty-handed. This allowance varies from bank to bank. And with respect to who gets paid for the transaction, the bank is the one that pays the real estate commissions.

The proper negotiation skills and documentation are required in order to have the correct presentation of the 'packet'. The lender must be able to quickly see that you qualify for a short sale.

Why would the bank not consider your property for a short sale?

If you have not made an effort to try to sell the property in a regular market before the request for short sale. Besides, you might have equity in your property. So why would you want to walk away from that equity?

If you can't afford your payments, that is not good enough reasons for the bank to accept your request.

If you lost your job, your wife, or health. All these are seen to the bank as temporary reasons.

Another big no-no is just because your property went down in value. It does not mean you payments have gone up: therefore, the bank has no reason to give you a short sale.

<u>Good reasons for the bank to let you short sale the property</u>

There could be a few reasons or many; it depends on your case manager at the bank.

The bank will study the property to see whether there is equity in your property; If there is, then yes.

The property is in good condition and location.

Your financial condition, age, health, and current situation. Most people would not agree with me, but I have worked in the foreclosure department at the bank and know firsthand how they process information.

Things to remember

You do not have to be late on the mortgage or missed a payment to qualify for sale in short sale. Your credit will never have to show late mortgage payments, and at the end of the sale you will show paid off in full. That is the reason why you should able to buy another property in the future.

<u>What is the benefit of the short sale for the seller?</u>

First of all, you will avoid foreclosure as well as the negative effects that it has on your credit.

Your credit will show "Paid in Full" once the transaction has been completed.

You can be back on your feet again and ready to purchase a new home within 6-12 months, if you desire and your situation permits.

The negative side of a short sale for seller

You will have to pay the IRS

Usually people are scared to sell their home in a short sale because they do not want to be responsible of owing money to the IRS. The bank writes off the loss and reports it. If you have concerns about dealing with the forgiven amount, you can speak about it with your CPA/ or Attorney. Remember, I am not a CPA or an attorney but can tell you that a CPA or your attorney can help you explain the situation to the IRS. The truth is your debt doesn't go away: it just changes forms. At completion of a short sale you may receive a 1099-C. Note: The Mortgage Debt Relief Act only applies to the 1099-C.

What are the benefits of a short sale for buyers?

You could buy a great property below-market

You do not have to rush to move in because usually, closing escrow takes longer than the traditional sale

Negative aspects of buying short sales

Your real estate agent must be able to follow directions on how to submit your offer to the bank otherwise, will take a long time to get a response.

The time it takes to close escrow on the property could be far more than a conventional transaction.

Usually, you'll be asked to buy the property "as is", which means no repairs, but that depends on the bank's representative in charge of the file. For the most part, they would not do any repairs other than the customary items because the bank is already losing money. The most you'll probably get is a home warranty policy and most likely not a pest, sewer inspection; roof certification; or money for closing costs.

The difference between buying a short sale and foreclosure

The difference between buying a short sale and foreclosure is usually with whom you have to deal with. In a short sale you have the owner of the property, the bank, and the real estate listing agent. In a foreclosure, you're no longer dealing with the owner of the property because the owner of the property now is the bank. It's better. The bank has money and when they have the property in their files they want to get rid of it. They spent money maintaining the property. It makes the changes necessary in order to sell property quickly. The bank might also take less time than if it would've been a short sale because it is losing money. You could get at a bargain price!

The difference between a 1099-C and a 1099-A

The 'C' stands for "Cancellation of Debt" and the 'A' stands for "Acquisition or Abandonment of Secured Property".

Another note worth mentioning is that with a 1099-C you must declare the forgiven amount as part of your annual income in the year you sold the house and with a 1099-A you may have to pay profit gains. For more details, consult with your tax advisor.

The Second mortgages

The first lien holder has the right to collect first. In a short sale, the first lien holder negotiates with the second lien holder. The second lien holder lets go the debt and gets compensated

Chapter 3

What is Foreclosure?

A foreclosure is a legal preceding that is started by a creditor (bank) to take possession of the collateral for a loan, which was agreed upon with the debtor when the loan is in default. But there are more threats than the consequences for not paying the mortgage. The tax assessor can also foreclose you for your lack of paying property taxes too. Additionally, your HOA (Home Owners Association) could foreclose you for not paying the monthly fee or yearly fees. Foreclosure procedures usually start after several missed payments like three or four. A foreclosure is governed by law, and it has to be carried out in accordance with the law governing it for it to be legal.

Types of foreclosures

Strict foreclosure is when the lender becomes the full owner of the property, by design when a borrower of the loan defaults.

Judicial foreclosure is also known as a public sale. The court usually comes to a decision on the title questions as well as approving each step of the bank foreclosure procedures. Then the government auctions off the property. In a home foreclosure procedure by a power of sale, the bank could sell the property under court supervision and does so freely.

Foreclosure through a deed in lieu.

The borrower may grant ownership of their property to the lender through a deed in lieu. The borrower loses the property but is forgiven the debt payment. The lender once in possession can sell the property to recoup the loss on the loan.

Tax Lien or Sheriff's Sales of Properties in foreclosure are those that have unpaid taxes and are delinquent.

HOA Foreclosure (Home Owners Associations). These associations are not required to go through a court to foreclose, as a property owner would evict a tenant. Neither homeowner receives the benefit of the homestead exemption when an association forecloses on their house, as they would in the case of any other money judgment.

Associations primarily use non-judicial foreclosure, which does not require review by a court.

How to Prevent Foreclosure Procedures

If you start experiencing financial difficulties, you should contact your bank, HOA, or County Tax Office immediately. In these situations, you must start planning, the sooner the better, for alternative options. If it is the bank, you could get a loan modification, deed–in-lieu, and some of the payments to the back of the loan and could also try to short sale the property. If it is your taxes, you could make an arrangement with the tax assessor to get a payment plan to avoid attorney fees and the accumulation of interests. If it is the HOA, then you could make arrangements for a payment plan to avoid attorney's fees and the accumulation of interests as well. It does not matter if you are current on your mortgage, the tax assessor or the homeowner's association could still foreclose your property. Usually included in your mortgage payment a portion goes for the property taxes which the bank pays every year. And even if you don't have an escrow account with your bank, the bank will still pay taxes to avoid foreclosure.

Chapter 4

HUD Homes

These are homes owned by the U.S. Department of Housing and Urban Development. They are sold through an electronic auction to the highest bidder. Buyers should expect to find properties in similar condition as bank owned homes.

A benefit of buying a HUD home is that the buying process is very well defined and with a very strict timeline. Homebuyers usually receive an answer within 24 hours of bid submission and a typical transaction closes between 45 and 55 days from the date when the bid was submitted.

The difference between HUD homes and Foreclosure

A HUD home is one that had an FHA Loan that foreclosed on. A Foreclosed Bank Owned homes or home is one that had a Conventional Loan that went sour that are being sold by a bank or other corporate lender! With a HUD you are dealing with U.S. Department of Housing and Urban Development and they do not negotiate, or make any repairs to the properties you buy "as is" with the privet bank you could negotiate for repairs and fees. You have more leverage with a conventional foreclosure.

Chapter 5

What is a Loan Modification?

A loan modification is an adjustment to the original terms agreed upon by the lender and the borrower. There are three areas that can be adjusted: Interest rates, the principal owed, and length of the loan. The outstanding principal owed is the one area a lender is less likely to want to modify, but in some cases they must negotiate this area with the borrower to make a modification work.

The most common reason a lender will consider modifying a mortgage is because the homeowner can no longer make the payments. There are a variety of reasons for this: 1) the homeowner lost his job, 2) a divorce, 3) adjustable mortgages, 4) the homeowner took out an equity line of credit, which they can't repay, 5) illness. These are some of the common ones.

In these cases, the lender, once the homeowner proves their situation is in bad shape, will consider a loan modification. It costs the lender a lot of money to foreclose on a property, so keeping the homeowner in the house is more cost effective in many cases. Since each situation is different, there is no way to pin down one type of modification. If the homeowner just needs time to catch up, then deferring payments for a period of time and attaching them to the back end of the loan could be the right modification for that person. Someone else may need a reduction in interest rates or even forgiveness of some of their principal owed. That is assessed on a case-by-case basis. Note. Loan modifications are not given to investors.

And It is also important to know the following: Banks will not offer modification options to lines of credit since it sees them like if they were credit cards. The reason behind it is that interest rates on those credits fluctuate.

Chapter 6

What is a reverse mortgage?

A reverse mortgage is a special type of home loan that lets you convert a portion of the equity in your home into cash. The equity that you built up over years of making mortgage payments can be paid to you. However, unlike a traditional home equity loan or second mortgage, HECM (Home Equity Conversion Mortgage) borrowers do not have to repay the HECM loan until the borrowers no longer use the home as their principal residence or fail to meet the obligations of the mortgage. You can also use an HECM to purchase a primary residence if you are able to use cash on hand to pay the difference between the HECM proceeds and the sales price plus closing costs for the property you are purchasing.

Requirements to get a reverse mortgage

Requires are that the homeowner must be 62 years of age or older, own the home outright, or have a low mortgage balance that can be paid off at closing.

Can I leave an estate to my heirs with proceeds from the reverse loan? Must I live in the home? I am pretty sure an HECM counselor can give more details on these questions and several more you might have, and there is also free information on reverse mortgages at the U.S. Department of Housing and Urban Development website.

What are the differences between a reverse mortgage and a home equity loan?

Borrowers must have adequate income to qualify for the loan, and they make monthly payments on the principal and interest. A reverse mortgage is different because it pays you – there are no monthly principal and interest payments. With a reverse mortgage, you are still required to pay real estate taxes, utilities, and hazard, and flood insurance premiums.

When the home is sold or no longer used as a primary residence, the cash, interest, and other HECM finance charges must be repaid. All proceeds beyond the amount owed belong to you. But if you have died, your spouse or estate will receive the proceeds. This means any remaining equity can be transferred to heirs. No debt is passed along to the estate or heirs.

How do I receive my payments?

You can select from five payment plans:

Tenure- equal monthly payments as long as at least one borrower lives and continues to occupy the property as a principal residence.

Term- equal monthly payments for a fixed period of months selected.

Line of Credit- unscheduled payments or in installments, at times and in an amount of your choosing until the line of credit is exhausted.

The modified Tenure – a combination of line of credit and scheduled monthly payments for as long as you remain in the home.

Modified Term- a combination of line of credit plus monthly payments for a fixed period of months selected by the borrower.

Chapter 7

What does "renting with an option to buy" mean?

How They Work: These agreements allow you to pay rent monthly on your apartment or house, with some or all of your payments being used to defray the cost of eventually buying it. Usually, you'll have a contract at the outset specifying how long you can rent and what portion of your payments count toward the down payment. Lease options can seem like the solution to your problems but easily turn into disasters. What you must know is that no two deals are alike, everything is negotiable, and the terms are much important than price. If you can't exercise your option, you usually lose your money and the rent credits unless otherwise agreed upon in writing.

Most buyers are only interested in a Lease Option because they can't get a loan due to no money and/or bad credit. MOST sellers accept Lease Options because their property is overpriced and MOST buyers seek Lease Options because they can't get a loan. Put the two of them together, and what do you get? The unqualified buyer contracts to purchase an overpriced property.

What happens when the above Lease Option is about to expire?

All hell breaks loose for everybody involved.

The real estate agents and buyers scramble from mortgage broker to mortgage broker, often they submit fraudulent loan applications.

There's a good chance that the property doesn't appraise at the seller price.

Sometimes the buyers give up and lose their option money and rent credits. Rarely will sellers grant a one-year extension so the buyers can get it together. Sometimes a funky deal is arranged with seller financing or an ARM. And there's the good chance the buyer\ will be by default a few years later. It's not impossible to structure a sensible lease option; I just rarely see it happen.

Chapter 8

Don't think it will be easier just to rent.

I do not know the situation across the country but can tell you how it is here in Texas for people who would like to rent. What the rental companies are requesting from the applicant in the screening criteria is quite tough as any loan underwriter would if it the applicant were trying to get a mortgage. Here's an example of what the common things rental companies are requesting from future tenants. And keep in mind that is not some of these things but all of these things that the applicant must submit.

Application Requirements/Qualifications:

Monthly income should be three times the rent amount and verifiable.

The rent amount cannot exceed 35% of the gross monthly income.

Applicant must submit savings or similar financial institution account statements showing a minimum balance maintained for the preceding six months equivalent to 12 months of rent payment.

Three of the most current pays stubs for anyone 18 years older. W2's is not accepted form of employment verification. They will accept 1099s if you're a business owner, however, they will need the last two years of 1099s to verify income.

Payments past due 60 days or more in the last 24 months may be caused for disapproval of the application.

They will run your credit (FICO 650+); do a background check to include criminal and eviction checks; and contact

previous landlords for rental history verification; they may even contact your current employer as well.

Applicants must list the last three landlord's information.

If the applicants are legally married, only one application processes fee is required. Common-law spouses, each roommate, and boy/ girlfriends that will be responsible for it rental payments must pay a separate application processing fee.

A $50 application fee for any occupant 18 years or older.

Legible copies of ID for anyone 18 years old or older.

A $300 pet deposit. Applicant must provide a photograph of the pet as well as taking the pet to the management office for an interview.

No smoking inside the home or garage.

Other reason you would be denied:

Unless there is a substantial security deposit, the applicant may be the denied if the applicant filed for bankruptcy within the last 36 months.

Unpaid collections within the last three years will result in denial of the application.

A federal tax lien is a reason for denial of the application.

If foreclosed in the last three years, the applicant will be disapproved.

If 20% or more of total accounts are past due, the applicant will be declined.

If applicant has written two or more NSF checks within the last 12 months.

If applicant allows person(s) not on the lease to reside in the premises, management may evict.

The applicant can no bring co-signers.

Remember all these requirements must comply with the Fair Housing Act. The law of equal opportunity housing dictates that there should not be discrimination based on creed, race, religion, gender, family, status, age, ancestry or public assistance status.

I do not know about you but I certainly do not want to be a renter. There is way too much intrusion.

So what is a person who cannot pay their mortgage to do?

Would they rather deal with a landlord or with the bank?

In my opinion, it is better to fight with the bank before losing the house than to fight with a landlord. The philosophy or rationale for most managing/rental companies these days is that if a person walk away from his/her mortgage, easily he/she could walk away from any rental lease.

Appendix A

Real Estate Terms and Definitions

Acceleration clause

A clause in your mortgage, which allows the lender to demand payment of the outstanding loan balance for various reasons. The most common reasons for accelerating a loan are if the borrower defaults on the loan or transfers title to another individual without informing the lender.

Adjustable-rate mortgage (ARM)

A mortgage in which the interest changes periodically, according to corresponding fluctuations in an index.

All ARM are tied to indexes.

Amortization

The loan payment consists of a portion, which will be applied to pay the accruing interest on a loan, with the remainder being applied to the principal. Over time, the interest portion decreases as the loan balance decreases, and the amount applied to principal increases so that the loan is paid off (amortized) in the specified time.

Annual percentage rate (APR)

This is not the note rate on your loan. It is a value created according to a government formula intended to reflect the true annual cost of borrowing, expressed as a percentage. It works sort of like this, but not exactly, so only use this as a guideline: deduct the closing costs from your loan amount, then using your actual loan payment, calculate what the interest rate would be on this amount instead of your actual loan amount. You will come up with a number close to the APR. Because you are using the same payment on a smaller amount, the APR is always higher than the actual rate on your loan.

Appraisal

A written justification of the price paid for a property, primarily based on an analysis of comparable sales of similar homes nearby.

Appraised value

An opinion of a property's fair market value, based on an appraiser's knowledge, experience, and analysis of the property. Since an appraisal is based primarily on comparable sales, and the most recent sale is the one on the property in question, the appraisal usually comes out at the purchase price.

Appreciation

The increase in the value of a property due to changes in market conditions, inflation, or other causes.

Assessed value

The valuation placed on a property by a public tax assessor for purposes of taxation.

Assignment

When ownership of your mortgage is transferred from one company or individual to another, it is called an assignment.

Assumable mortgage

A mortgage that can be assumed by the buyer when a home is sold. Usually, the borrower must "qualify" in order to assume the loan.

Assumption

The term applied when a buyer assumes the seller's mortgage.

Balloon mortgage

A mortgage loan that requires the remaining principal balance be paid at a specific point in time. For example, a loan may be amortized as if it would be paid over a thirty-year period, but requires that at the end of the tenth year the entire remaining balance must be paid.

Bill of sale

A written document that transfers title to personal property. For example, when selling an automobile to acquire funds, which will be used as a source of down payment or for closing costs, the lender will usually require the bill of sale (in addition to other items) to help document this source of funds.

Biweekly mortgage

A mortgage in which you make payments every two weeks instead of once a month. The basic result is that instead of making twelve monthly payments during the year, you make thirteen. The extra payment reduces the principal, substantially reducing the time it takes to pay off a thirty-year mortgage. *Note:* there are independent companies that encourage you to set up bi-weekly payment schedules with them on your thirty-year mortgage. They charge a set-up fee and a transfer fee for every payment. Your funds are deposited into a trust account from which your monthly payment is then made and the excess funds then remain in the trust account until enough has accrued to make the additional payment, which will then be paid to reduce your principle. You could save money by doing the same thing yourself, plus you have to have faith that once you transfer money to them that they will actually transfer your funds to your lender.

Bridge loan

Not used much anymore, bridge loans are obtained by those who have not yet sold their previous property but must close on a purchase property. The bridge loan becomes the source of their funds for the down payment. One reason for their fall from favor is that there are more and more second mortgage lenders now that will lend at a high loan to value. In addition, sellers often prefer to accept offers from buyers who have already sold their property.

Buy down

Usually refers to a fixed rate mortgage where the interest rate is "bought down" for a temporary period, usually one to three years. After that time and for the remainder of the term, the borrower's payment is calculated at the note rate. In order to buy down the initial rate for the temporary payment, a lump sum is paid and held in an account used to supplement the borrower's monthly payment. These funds usually come from the seller (or some other source) as a financial incentive to induce someone to buy their property. A "lender funded buy down" is when the lender pays the initial lump sum. They can accomplish this because the note rate on the loan (after the buy down adjustments) will be higher than the current market rate. One reason for doing this is because the borrower may get to "qualify" at the start rate and can qualify for a higher loan amount. Another reason is that a borrower may expect his earnings to go up substantially in the near future, but wants a lower payment right now.

Cap

Adjustable Rate Mortgages have fluctuating interest rates, but those fluctuations are usually limited to a certain amount. Those limitations may apply to how much the loan may adjust over a six-month period, an annual period, and over the life of the loan, and are referred to as "caps." Some ARM, although they may have a life cap, allow the interest rate to fluctuate freely, but require a certain minimum payment, which can change once a year. There is a limit on how much that payment can change each year, and that limit is also referred to as a cap.

Cash-out refinance

When a borrower refinances his mortgage at a higher amount than the current loan balance with the intention of pulling out money for personal use, it is referred to as "cash out refinance."

Chain of title

An analysis of the transfers of title to a piece of property over the years.

Clear title

A title that is free of liens or legal questions as to ownership of the property.

Closing costs

Closing costs are separated into what are called "non-recurring closing costs" and "pre-paid items." Nonrecurring closing costs are any items, which are paid just once as a result of buying the property or obtaining a loan. "Pre-paid" are items, which recur over time, such as property taxes and homeowner's insurance. A lender makes an attempt to estimate the amount of non-recurring closing costs and prepaid items on the Good Faith Estimate, which they must issue to the borrower within three days of receiving a home loan application.

Cloud on title

Any conditions revealed by a title search that adversely affect the title to real estate. Usually, clouds on title cannot be removed except by deed, release, or court action.

Collection

When a borrower falls behind, the lender contacts them in an effort to bring the loan current. The loan goes to "collection." As part of the collection effort, the lender must mail and record certain documents in case they are eventually required to foreclose on the property.

Common - area assessments

In some areas, they are called Homeowners Association Fees. They are charges paid to the Homeowners Association by the owners of the individual units in a condominium or planned unit development (PUD) and are generally used to maintain the property and common areas.

Common areas

Those portions of a building, land, and amenities owned (or managed) by a planned unit development (PUD) or condominium project's homeowners' association (or a cooperative project's cooperative corporation) that are used by all of the unit owners, who share in the common expenses of their operation and maintenance. Common areas include swimming pools, tennis courts, and other recreational facilities, as well as common corridors of buildings, parking areas, means of ingress and egress, etc.

Comparable sales

Recent sales of similar properties in nearby areas and used to help determine the market value of a property. Also referred to as "comps."

Construction loan

A short-term, interim loan for financing the cost of construction. The lender makes payments to the builder at periodic intervals as the work progresses.

Contingency

A condition that must be met before a contract is legally binding. For example, home purchasers often include a contingency that specifies that the contract is not binding until the purchaser obtains a satisfactory home inspection report from a qualified home inspector.

Conventional mortgage

Refers to home loans other than government loans (VA and FHA).

Convertible ARM

An adjustable-rate mortgage that allows the borrower to change the ARM to a fixed-rate mortgage within a specific time.

Cooperative (co-op)

A type of multiple ownership in which the residents of a multiunit housing complex own shares in the cooperative corporation that owns the property, giving each resident the right to occupy a specific apartment or unit.

Deed

The legal document conveying title to a property.

Deed-in-lieu

Short for "deed in lieu of foreclosure," this conveys title to the lender when the borrower is in default and wants to avoid foreclosure. The lender may or may not cease foreclosure activities if a borrower asks to provide a deed-in-lieu. Regardless of whether the lender accepts the deed-in-lieu, the avoidance and non-repayment of debt will most likely show on a credit history. What a deed-in-lieu may prevent is having the documents preparatory to a foreclosure being recorded and become a matter of public record.

Deed of trust

Some states, like California, do not record mortgages. Instead, they record a deed of trust, which is essentially the same thing.

Default

Failure to make the mortgage payment within a specified period of time. For first mortgages or first trust deeds, if a payment has still not been made within 30 days of the due date, the loan is considered to be in default.

Delinquency

Failure to make mortgage payments when mortgage payments are due. For most mortgages, on the first day of the month. Even though they may not charge a "late fee" for a number of days, the payment is still considered to be late and the loan delinquent. When a loan payment is more than 30 days late, most lenders report the late payment to one or more credit bureaus.

Depreciation

A decline in the value of property; the opposite of appreciation. Depreciation is also an accounting term, which shows the declining monetary value of an asset and is used as an expense to reduce taxable income. Since this is not a true expense where money is actually paid, lenders will add back depreciation expense for self-employed borrowers and count it as income.

Due-on-sale provision

A provision in a mortgage that allows the lender to demand repayment in full if the borrower sells the property that serves as security for the mortgage.

Earnest money deposit

A deposit made by the potential homebuyer to show that he or she is serious about buying the house.

Eminent domain

The right of a government to take private property for public use upon payment of its fair market value. Eminent domain is the basis for condemnation proceedings.

Equal Credit Opportunity Act (ECOA)

A federal law that requires lenders and other creditors to make credit equally available without discrimination based on race, color, religion, national origin, age, sex, marital status, or receipt of income from public assistance programs.

Equity

A homeowner's financial interest in a property. Equity is the difference between the fair market value of the property and the amount still owed on its mortgage and other liens.

Escrow

An item of value, money, or documents deposited with a third party to be delivered upon the fulfillment of a condition. For example, the earnest money deposit is put into escrow until delivered to the seller when the transaction is closed.

Escrow account

Once you close your purchase transaction, you may have an escrow account or impound account with your lender. This means the amount you pay each month includes an amount above what would be required if you were only paying your principal and interest. The extra money is held in yours impound account (escrow account) for the payment of items like property taxes and homeowner's insurance when they come due. The lender pays them with your money instead of you paying them yourself.

Escrow disbursements

The use of escrow funds to pay real estate taxes, hazard insurance, mortgage insurance, and other property expenses as they become due.

Eviction

The lawful expulsion of an occupant from real property.

Examination of title

The report on the title of a property from the public records or an abstract of the title.

Executor

A person named in a will to administer an estate. The court will appoint an administrator if no executor is named. "Executrix" is the feminine form.

Fair Credit Reporting Act

A consumer protection law that regulates the disclosure of consumer credit reports by consumer/credit reporting agencies and establishes procedures for correcting mistakes on one's credit record.

Fair market value

The highest price that a buyer, willing but not compelled to buy would pay, and the lowest a seller, willing but not compelled to sell, would accept.

Fannie Mae (FNMA)

The Federal National Mortgage Association, which is a congressionally chartered, shareholder-owned company that is the nation's largest supplier of home mortgage funds. For a discussion of the roles of Fannie Mae, Freddie Mac (FHLMC), and Ginnie Mae (GNMA), sees the Library.

Fannie Mae's Community Home Buyer's Program

An income-based community lending model, under which mortgage insurers and Fannie Mae offer flexible underwriting guidelines to increase a low or moderate-income family's buying power and to decrease the total amount of cash needed to purchase a home. Borrowers who participate in this model are required to attend pre-purchase homebuyer education sessions.

Federal Housing Administration (FHA)

An agency of the U.S. Department of Housing and Urban Development (HUD). Its main activity is the insuring of residential mortgage loans made by private lenders. The FHA sets standards for construction and underwriting but does not lend money or plan or construct housing.

Fee simple

The greatest possible interest a person can have in real estate.

Fee simple estate

An unconditional, unlimited estate of inheritance that represents the greatest estate and most extensive interest in land that can be enjoyed. It is of perpetual duration. When the real estate is in a condominium project, the unit owner is the exclusive owner only of the air space within his or her portion of the building (the unit) and is an owner in common with respect to the land and other common portions of the property.

FHA mortgage

A mortgage that is insured by the Federal Housing Administration (FHA). Along with VA loans, an FHA loan will often be referred to as a government loan.

Firm commitment

A lender's agreement to make a loan to a specific borrower on a specific property.

First mortgage

The mortgage that is in first place among any loans recorded against a property. Usually, refers to the date in which loans are recorded, but there are exceptions.

Fixed-rate mortgage

A mortgage in which the interest rate does not change during the entire term of the loan.

Foreclosure

The legal process by which a borrower in default under a mortgage is deprived of his or her interest in the mortgaged property. This usually involves a forced sale of the property at public auction with the proceeds of the sale being applied to the mortgage debt.

Government loan (mortgage)

A mortgage that is insured by the Federal Housing Administration (FHA) or guaranteed by the Department of Veterans Affairs (VA) or the Rural Housing Service (RHS). Mortgages that are not government loans are classified as conventional loans.

Government National Mortgage Association

(Ginnie Mae)

A government-owned corporation within the U.S. Department of Housing and Urban Development (HUD). Created by Congress on September 1, 1968, GNMA performs the same role as Fannie Mae and Freddie Mac in providing funds to lenders for making home loans. The difference is that Ginnie Mae provides funds for government loans (FHA and VA)

Grantee

The person to whom an interest in real property is conveyed.

Grantor

The person conveying an interest in real property.

Home Equity Conversion Mortgage (HECM)

Usually referred to as a reverse annuity mortgage, what makes this type of mortgage unique is that instead of making payments to a lender, the lender makes payments to you. It enables older homeowners to convert the equity they have in their homes into cash, usually in the form of monthly payments. Unlike traditional home equity loans, a borrower does not qualify on the basis of income but on the value of his or her home. In addition, the loan does not have to be repaid until the borrower no longer occupies the property.

payments are due **Home equity line of credit**

A mortgage loan, usually in second position, that allows the borrower to obtain cash drawn against the equity of his home, up to a predetermined amount.

Homeowners' association

A nonprofit association that manages the common areas of a planned unit development (PUD) or condominium project. In a condominium project, it has no ownership interest in the common elements. In a PUD project, it holds title to the common elements.

Homeowner's insurance

An insurance policy that combines personal liability insurance and hazard insurance coverage for a dwelling and its contents.

Homeowner's warranty

A type of insurance often purchased by homebuyers that will cover repairs to certain items, such as heating or air conditioning, should they break down within the coverage period. The buyer often requests the seller to pay for this coverage as a condition of the sale, but either party can pay.

HUD median income

Median family income for a particular county or metropolitan statistical area (MSA), as estimated by the Department of Housing and Urban Development (HUD).

HUD-1 settlement statement

A document that provides an itemized listing of the funds paid at closing. Items that appear on the statement include real estate commissions, loan fees, points, and initial escrow (impound) amounts. Each type of expense goes on a specific numbered line on the sheet. The totals at the bottom of the HUD-1 statement define the seller's net proceeds and the buyer's net payment at closing. It is called an HUD1 because the form is printed by the Department of Housing and Urban Development (HUD). The HUD1 statement is also known as the "closing statement" or "settlement sheet."

Joint tenancy

A form of ownership or taking title to property, which means each party, owns the whole property and that ownership is not separate. In the event of the death of one party, the survivor owns the property in its entirety.

Judgment

A decision made by a court of law. In judgments that require the repayment of a debt, the court may place a lien against the debtor's real property as collateral for the judgment's creditor. An alternative spelling is "judgment."

Judicial foreclosure

A type of foreclosure proceeding used in some states that are handled as a civil lawsuit and conducted entirely under the auspices of a court. Other states use non-judicial foreclosure.

Jumbo loan

A loan that exceeds Fannie Mae and Freddie Mac loan limits, currently at $227,150. Also called a nonconforming loan. Freddie Mac and Fannie Mae loans are referred to as conforming loans.

Lease

A written agreement between the property owner and a tenant that stipulates the payment and conditions under which the tenant may possess the real estate for a specified period of time.

Leasehold estate

A way of holding title to a property wherein the mortgagor does not actually own the property but rather has a recorded long-term lease on it.

Lease option

An alternative financing option that allows homebuyers to lease a home with an option to buy.

Each month's rent payment may consist of not only the rent but also an additional amount, which can be applied toward the down payment on an already specified price.

Legal description

A property description, recognized by law that is sufficient to locate and identify the property without oral testimony.

Lender

A term, which can refer to the institution making the loan or to the individual representing the firm. For example, loan officers are often referred to as "lenders."

Liabilities

A person's financial obligations. Liabilities include long-term and short-term debt, as well as any other amounts that are owed to others.

Lien

A legal claim against a property that must be paid off when the property is sold. A mortgage or first trust deed is considered a lien.

Life cap

For an adjustable-rate mortgage (ARM), a limit on the amount that the interest rate can increase or decrease over the life of the mortgage.

Line of credit

An agreement by a commercial bank or other financial institution to extend credit up to a certain amount for a certain time to a specified borrower.

Loan

A sum of borrowed money (principal) that is generally repaid with interest.

Loan officer

Also referred to by a variety of other terms, such as lender, loan representative, loan "rep," account executive, and others. The loan officer serves several functions and has various responsibilities: they solicit loans, they are the representatives of the lending institution, and they represent the borrower to the lending institution.

Loan origination

How a lender refers to the process of obtaining new loans.

Loan servicing

After you obtain a loan, the company you make the payments to is "servicing" your loan. They process payments, send statements, manage the escrow/impound account, provide collection efforts on delinquent loans, ensure that insurance and property taxes are made on the property, handle payoffs and assumptions, and provide a variety of other services.

Loan-to-value (LTV)

The percentage relationship between the amount of the loan and the appraised value or sales price (whichever is lower).

Lock-in

An agreement in which the lender guarantees a specified interest rate for a certain amount of time at a certain cost.

Lock-in period

The time period during which the lender has guaranteed an interest rate to a borrower.

Margin

The difference between the interest rate and the index on an adjustable rate mortgage. The margin remains stable over the life of the loan. It is the index, which moves up and down.

Maturity

The date on which the principal balance of a loan, bond, or other financial instrument becomes due and payable.

Modification

Occasionally, a lender will agree to modify the terms of your mortgage without requiring you t refinance. If any changes are made, it is called a modification.

Mortgage

A legal document that pledges a property to the lender as security for payment of a debt. Instead of mortgages, some states use First Trust Deeds.

Mortgage banker

For a complete discussion of a mortgage banker, see "Types of Lenders." A mortgage banker is generally assumed to originate and fund its own loans, which are then sold on the secondary market, usually to Fannie Mae, Freddie Mac, or Ginnie Mae. However, firms rather loosely apply this term to themselves, whether they are true mortgage bankers or simply mortgage brokers or correspondents.

Mortgage insurance (MI)

Insurance that covers the lender against some of the losses incurred as a result of a default on a home loan. Often mistake one of the larger mortgage insurers. Mortgage insurance is usually required in one form or another on all loans that have a loan-to-value higher than eighty percent. Mortgages above 80% LTV that call themselves "No MI" are usually a made at a higher interest rate. Instead of the borrower paying the mortgage insurance premiums directly, they pay a higher interest rate to the lender, which then pays the mortgage insurance. Also, FHA loans and certain first-time homebuyer programs require mortgage insurance regardless of the loan-to-value.

Mortgage insurance premium (MIP)

The amount paid by a mortgagor for mortgage insurance, either to a government agency such as the Federal Housing Administration (FHA) or to a private mortgage insurance (MI) company.

Mortgage life and disability insurance

A type of term life insurance often bought by borrowers. The amount of coverage decreases as the principal balance declines. Some policies also cover the borrower in the event of disability. In the event that the borrower dies, while the policy is in force, the debt is automatically satisfied by insurance proceeds. In the case of disability insurance, the insurance will make the mortgage payment for a specified amount of time during the disability. Be careful to read the terms of coverage, however, because often the coverage does not start immediately upon the disability, but after a specified period, sometimes forty-five days.

Mortgagor

The borrower in a mortgage agreement.

Multi-dwelling units

Properties that provide separate housing units for more than one family, although they secure only a single mortgage.

Negative amortization

Some adjustable rate mortgages allow the interest rate to fluctuate independently of a required minimum payment. If a borrower makes the minimum payment it may not cover all of the interest that would normally be due at the current interest rate. In essence, the borrower is deferring the interest payment, which is why this is called "deferred interest." The deferred interest is added to the balance of the loan and the loan balance grows larger instead of smaller, which is called negative amortization.

No cash-out refinance

A refinance transaction which is not intended to put cash in the hand of the borrower. Instead, the new balance is calculated to cover the balance due on the current loan and any costs associated with obtaining the new mortgage. Often referred to as a "rate and term refinance."

No-cost loan

Many lenders offer loans that you can obtain at "no cost." You should inquire whether this means there are no "lender" costs associated with the loan, or if it also covers the other costs you would normally have in a purchase or refinance transactions, such as title insurance, escrow fees, settlement fees, appraisal, recording fees, notary fees, and others. These are fees and costs, which may be associated with buying a home or obtaining a loan, but not charged directly by the lender. Keep in mind that, like a "no-point" loan, the interest rate will be higher than if you obtain a loan that has costs associated with it.

Note

A legal document that obligates a borrower to repay a mortgage loan at a stated interest rate during a specified period of time.

Note rate

The interest rate stated on a mortgage note.

No-point loan

Almost all lenders offer loans at "no-points." You will find the interest rate on a "no points" loan is approximately a quarter percent higher than on a loan where you pay one point.

Notice of default

A formal written notice to a borrower that a default has occurred and that legal action may be taken.

Original principal balance

The total amount of principal owed on a mortgage before any payments are made.

Origination fee

On a government loan, the loan origination fee is one percent of the loan amount, but additional points may be charged which are called "discount points." One point equals one percent of the loan amount. On a conventional loan, the loan origination fee refers to the total number of points a borrower pays.

Owner financing

A property purchase transaction in which the property seller provides all or part of the financing.

Partial payment

A payment that is not sufficient to cover the scheduled monthly payment on a mortgage loan. Normally, a lender will not accept a partial payment, but in times of hardship, you can make this request of the loan servicing collection department.

Payment change date

The date when a new monthly payment amount takes effect on an adjustable-rate mortgage (ARM) or a graduated-payment mortgage (GPM). Generally, the payment change date occurs in the month immediately after the interest rate adjustment date.

Periodic rate cap

For an adjustable-rate mortgage, a limit on the amount that the interest rate can increase or decrease during any one-adjustment period, regardless of how high or low the index might be.

Personal property

Any property that is not real property.

PITI

This stands for principal, interest, taxes and insurance. If you have an "impounded" loan, then your monthly payment to the lender includes all of these and probably includes mortgage insurance as well. If you do not have an impounded account, then the lender still calculates this amount and uses it as part of determining your debt-to-income ratio.

PITI reserves

A cash amount that a borrower must have on hand after making a down payment and paying all closing costs for the purchase of a home. The principal, interest, taxes, and insurance (PITI) reserves must equal the amount that the borrower would have to pay for PITI for a predefined number of months.

Planned unit development (PUD)

A type of ownership where individuals actually own the building or unit they live in, but common areas are owned jointly with the other members of the development or association. Contrast with condominium, where an individual actually owns the airspace of his unit, but the buildings and common areas are owned jointly with the others in the development or association.

Point

A point is 1 percent of the amount of the mortgage.

Power of attorney

A legal document that authorizes another person to act on one's behalf. A power of attorney can grant complete authority or can be limited to certain acts and/or certain periods of time.

Pre-approval

A loosely used term which is generally taken to mean that a borrower has completed a loan application and provided debt, income, and savings documentation which an underwriter has reviewed and approved. A pre-approval is usually done at a certain loan amount and making assumptions about what the interest rate will actually be at the time the loan is actually made, as well as estimates for the amount that will be paid for property taxes, insurance, and others. A pre-approval applies only to the borrower. Once a property is chosen, it must also meet the underwriting guidelines of the lender. Contrast with pre-qualification.

Prepayment

Any amount paid to reduce the principal balance of a loan before the due date. Payment in full on a mortgage that may result from a sale of the property, the owner's decision to pay off the loan in full, or a foreclosure. In each case, prepayment means payment occurs before the loan has been fully amortized.

Prepayment penalty

A fee that may be charged to a borrower who pays off a loan before it is due.

Pre-qualification

This usually refers to the loan officer's written opinion of the ability of a borrower to qualify for a home loan, after the loan officer has made inquiries about debt, income, and savings. The information provided to the loan officer may have been presented verbally or in the form of documentation, and the loan officer may or may not have reviewed a credit report on the borrower.

Prime rate

The interest rates that banks charge to their preferred customers. Changes in the prime rate are widely publicized in the news media and are used as the indexes in some adjustable rate mortgages, especially home equity lines of credit. Changes in the prime rate do not directly affect other types of mortgages, but the same factors that influence the prime rate also affect the interest rates on mortgage loans.

Principal

The amount borrowed or remaining unpaid. The part of the monthly payment that reduces the remaining balance of a mortgage.

Principal balance

The outstanding balance of principal on a mortgage. The principal balance does not include interest or any other charges. See remaining balance.

Principal, interest, taxes, and insurance (PITI)

The four components of a monthly mortgage payment on impounded loans. The principal refers to the part of the monthly payment that reduces the remaining balance of the mortgage. Interest is the fee charged for borrowing money. Taxes and insurance refer to the amounts that are paid into an escrow account each month for property taxes and mortgage and hazard insurance.

Private mortgage insurance (MI)

Mortgage insurance that is provided by a private mortgage insurance company to protect lenders against loss if a borrower defaults. Most lenders generally require MI for a loan with a loan-to-value (LTV) percentage in excess of 80 percent.

Promissory note

A written promise to repay a specified amount over a specified period of time.

Public auction

A meeting in an announced public location to sell the property to repay a mortgage that is in default.

Planned Unit Development (PUD)

A project or subdivision that includes common property that is owned and maintained by a homeowners' association for the benefit and use of the individual PUD unit owners.

Purchase agreement

A written contract signed by the buyer and seller stating the terms and conditions under which a property will be sold.

Qualifying ratios

Calculations that are used in determining whether a borrower can qualify for a mortgage. There are two ratios. The "top" or "front" ratio is a calculation of the borrower's monthly housing costs (principle, taxes, insurance, mortgage insurance, homeowner's association fees) as a percentage of monthly income. The "back" or "bottom" ratio includes housing costs as well as all other monthly debt.

Quitclaim deed

A deed that transfers without warranty whatever interest or title a grantor may have at the time the conveyance is made.

Rate lock

A commitment issued by a lender to a borrower or other mortgage originator guaranteeing a specified interest rate for a specified period of time at a specific cost.

Real estate agent

A person licensed to negotiate and transact the sale of real estate.

Real Estate Settlement Procedures Act (RESPA)

A consumer protection law that requires lenders to give borrowers advance notice of closing costs.

Real property

Land and appurtenances, including anything of a permanent nature such as structures, trees, minerals, and the interest, benefits, and inherent rights thereof.

Recorder

The public official who keeps records of transactions

that affects real property in the area. Sometimes known

as a "Registrar of Deeds" or "County Clerk."

Recording

The noting in the registrar's office of the details of a

properly executed the legal documents, such as a deed, a mortgage note, a satisfaction of mortgage, or an extension of mortgage, thereby making it a part of the public record.

Refinance transaction

The process of paying off one loan with the proceeds from a new loan using the same property as security.

Remaining balance

The amount of principal that has not yet been repaid. See principal balance.

Remaining term

The original amortization term minus the number of payments that have been applied.

Replacement reserve fund

A fund set aside for replacement of common property in a condominium, PUD, or cooperative project -- particularly that which has a short life expectancy, such as carpeting, furniture, etc.

Right of first refusal

A provision in an agreement that requires the owner of a property to give another party the first opportunity to purchase or lease the property before he or she offers it for sale or lease to others.

Right of ingress or egress

The right to enter or leave designated premises.

Right of survivorship

In joint tenancy, the right of survivors to acquire the interest of a deceased joint tenant.

Sale-leaseback

A technique in which a seller deeds the property to a buyer for a consideration and the buyer simultaneously leases the property back to the seller.

Second mortgage

A mortgage that has a lien position subordinate to the first mortgage.

Secondary market

The buying and selling of existing mortgages, usually as part of a "pool" of mortgages.

Secured loan

A loan that is backed by collateral.

Seller carry-back

An agreement in which the owner of a property provides financing, often in combination with an assumable mortgage.

Service

An organization that collects principal and interest payments from borrowers and manages borrowers' escrow accounts. The servicer often services mortgages that have been purchased by an investor in the secondary mortgage market.

Servicing

The collection of mortgage payments from borrowers and related responsibilities of a loan service.

Settlement statement

See HUD1 Settlement Statement

Subdivision

A housing development that is created by dividing a tract of land into individual lots for sale or lease.

Subordinate financing

Any mortgage or another lien that has a priority that is lower than that of the first mortgage.

Survey

A drawing or map showing the precise legal boundaries of a property, the location of improvements, easements, rights of way, encroachments, and other physical features.

Tenancy in common

As opposed to joint tenancy, when there are two or more individuals on title to a piece of property, this type of ownership does not pass ownership to the others in the event of death.

Third-party origination

A process by which a lender uses another party to completely or partially originate, process, underwrite, close, fund, or package the mortgages it plans to deliver to the secondary mortgage market.

Title

A legal document evidencing a person's right to or ownership of a property.

Title company

A company that specializes in examining and insuring titles to real estate.

Title insurance

Insurance that protects the lender (lender's policy) or the buyer (owner's policy) against loss arising from disputes over ownership of a property.

Title search

A check of the title records to ensure that the seller is the legal owner of the property and that there are no liens or other claims outstanding.

Transfer of ownership

Any means by which the ownership of a property changes hands. Lenders consider all of the following situations to be a transfer of ownership: the purchase of a property "subject to" the mortgage, the assumption of the mortgage debt by the property purchaser, and any exchange of possession of the property under a land sales contract or any other land trust device.

Transfer tax

State or local tax payable when title passes from one owner to another.

Two-step mortgage

An adjustable-rate mortgage (ARM) that has one interest rate for the first five or seven years of its mortgage term and a different interest rate for the remainder of the amortization term.

Two-four family property

A property that consists of a structure that provides living space (dwelling units) for two to four families, although ownership of the structure is evidenced by a single deed.

Trustee

A fiduciary who holds or controls property for the benefit of another.

VA mortgage

A mortgage that is guaranteed by the Department of Veterans Affairs (VA).

Vested

Having the right to use a portion of a fund such as an individual retirement fund. For example, individuals who are 100 percent vested can withdraw all of the funds that are set aside for them in a retirement fund. However, taxes may be due on any funds that are actually withdrawn.

Veterans Administration (VA)

An agency of the federal government that guarantees residential mortgages made to eligible veterans of the military services. The guarantee protects the lender against loss and thus encourages lenders to make mortgages to veterans.

Appendix B

References information

Real Estate abc.com Foreclosure
Procedures. COM What Is A Loan
Modification. net
U.S. Department of Housing and Urban Development
Buyhouse.net

We invite you to become a member and connect:

SUCASAOCASTILLO CHANNEL @ YouTube

http://www.youtube.com/user/sucasaocastillo/featured

Ariana CP Hunter is one of the few Hispanic,
female Real Estate Broker in Texas. She
holds several license and certification in various
disciplines. Ariana is the host of "Su Casa o
Castillo" Real Estate Show.

www.ingramcontent.com/pod-product-compliance
Lightning Source LLC
Chambersburg PA
CBHW051221170526
45166CB00005B/1995